Coastal walks around
Anglesey–*Volume 2*

On Holyhead Mountain above Gogarth, Holy Island

Coastal walks around
Anglesey–*Volume 2*

*15 circular walks around the Anglesey Coast
Area of Outstanding Natural Beauty*

Carl Rogers

MARA BOOKS

First published in June 1998 by **Mara Books**,
22 Crosland Terrace, Helsby, Cheshire WA6 9LY.
Telephone: 01928 723744

This new fully revised edition published by
Mara Books, March 2006.

ISBN 0 9522409 5 5

All enquiries regarding sales, telephone: (01928) 723744

Acknowledgements

I would like to thank Bob Nash for checking all the routes and Rosie Frankland of the Isle of Anglesey Coastal Path Project for the use of the photograph on page 40.

Layout and design by Mara Books.
Text, maps and photographs © Carl Rogers 2006

Contents

Introduction

THIS book is intended as a companion volume to *'Coastal Walks around Anglesey Volume 1'*, originally published way back in 1996. An instant success, the book has been revised and reprinted many times. It features a collection of walks which centre on what, in the author's opinion, are the finest walking areas around Anglesey's wild and beautiful coastline, one of Wales' five Areas of Outstanding Natural Beauty (AONB). At the same time care was taken to spread the walks evenly around the coast to sample as much of the island's varied scenery as possible.

Because of this there were many excellent routes which did not find their way into print in that first volume. *'Coastal Walks around Anglesey Volume 2'* is the result. One major difference with this second volume is that I have felt less obliged to avoid routes which use paths subject to tides. Thus, six of the walks require at least some thought to the timing of the walk and the state of the

Walking along the marsh edge, Newborough Warren

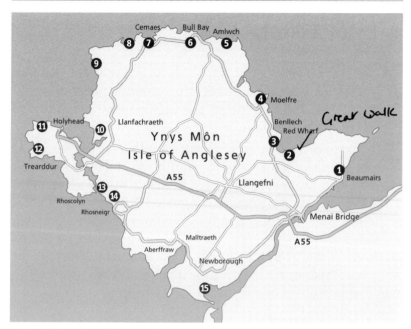

tide. This should not, however, be seen as making the walks dangerous in any way—a quick reference to local tide tables, (which are readily available almost anywhere on the island), is all the preparation you will need to make. This simple precaution should, however, not be ignored. Where possible, high tide alternatives have been included should you be in any doubt.

Perhaps the biggest change since the original volumes were published is the creation of the Isle of Anglesey Coastal Path which provides an almost continuous walking route around the entire island. The main impact of this is that the coastal sections of the walks have been vastly improved, with increased use and waymarking, and you should experience no problems in using these sections. Paths which adjoin the coastal path have also been improved, so many of the return loops are now far easier to follow and walk. But don't let all this talk of improvement, increased use and formalisation put you off, Anglesey can absorb a large number of walkers and on most of the routes you are likely to have just yourself for company.

A brief history of Anglesey

A NGLESEY has a rich historic heritage with visible remains of settlement reaching back into the second millennium BC. In fact the island has one of the highest concentrations of prehistoric sites in Britain.

The position of Anglesey, thrust out into the Irish Sea, along with its gentle terrain and the rich fertile soil of the interior, have ensured that it has been populated from the earliest times. In the 1,500 years before the Romans conquered Britain, various tribes settled in these islands and their method of travel, both for exploration and trade, seems to have been primarily by sea. As such, Anglesey was ideally placed at a crucial point in the seaways of western Britain. Unfortunately, this has also made it vulnerable to attack and invasion, which became a major feature of its early history.

The fact that Anglesey was densely populated in prehistoric times is made evident by large numbers of megalithic tombs, which provide the earliest visible remains of settlement on the island. Fine examples can be seen in the fields near Traeth Lligwy and Rhosneigr. Visitors to the restored burial chamber known as Bryn Celli Ddu near Llanddaniel Fab, can see the original form of these monuments.

The next phase of settlement—known as the Bronze Age— brought immigrants who have come to be known as the 'Beaker folk' (from their distinctive pottery) to Anglesey towards the end of the second millennium BC. It was these tribes who raised the island's many standing stones, although their purpose remains a mystery.

By the fifth century BC, Celtic tribes had begun to move into Britain and by the time of the Roman conquest, Anglesey is thought to have been one of the most important centres for the Celtic or 'old religion' in Britain and possibly even Europe. The writings of Julius Caesar suggest that the Druid religion was

Bronze Age standing stones at Penrhos Feilw

developed in Britain and exported to other Celtic tribes in Northern Europe. If this is true, Anglesey would have been one of the most important religious centres in Europe

This religion was taught by a class of priests known as 'Druids' and it seems to have been they who stirred up the greatest resistance to the Roman occupation of Britain. There seems little doubt that it was to stamp out this seat of spiritual resistance, that the Roman leader Suetonius Paulinus set out to invade

Lligwy Burial Chamber

Anglesey in AD 61. With an army of over 10,000, he crossed the Menai Strait and in one easily won battle extinguished the old Celtic religion completely. The sacred groves were destroyed and the Druid priesthood wiped out.

The fact that so little is now known about the Druids and indeed about much of the early history of the Celts, is due to the fact that they committed nothing to writing; all their religious teaching and history was passed on orally. All manner of fanciful and gruesome practices have been attributed to the Druids but nothing is really known about them for sure. Their knowledge and traditions died with them on the shores of the Menai Strait almost 2,000 years ago.

It was the Celts who introduced the Iron Age culture to Britain and their most enduring legacy is the many hillforts which can be seen all over the country. Anglesey is no exception and a number are visible today, with fine examples at Holyhead Mountain and Bwrdd Arthur. Perhaps the most impressive remains from this period are to be found at Din Lligwy near Moelfre. Here the visitor needs little imagination to visualise the settlement as it was—hut bases, doorways and enclosure walls are all clearly visible.

Despite its length—over 300 years—the Roman occupation left surprisingly few remains on Anglesey, which was probably controlled from the fort across the Menai Strait at Caernarfon (Segontium). The most notable remains are to be found at

British settlement at Din Lligwy

Holyhead, where the walls of a coastal fort still enclose St Cybi's church and the base of a lookout tower—known as Caer y Twr—stands inside the old hillfort on Holyhead Mountain.

If you stand on this summit today, you will enjoy a fine view out to sea in all directions, but on a clear evening out to the west you will see the Wicklow Mountains of southern Ireland, and it was from here, when the protective arm of Rome had been removed, that raiders came in the early post-Roman era. These invasions inevitably resulted in settlement and it may be significant that the hut circles on Holyhead Mountain are known today as 'Cytiau'r Gwyddelod' or the 'Irishmen's Huts'.

The Irish invasion became such a problem that a powerful Celtic chieftain or Romanised Celt from Strathclyde, came to North Wales with a large army commanded by his sons and devoted the rest of his life to ridding the land of these invaders. His name was Cunedda and it was in a last battle on Anglesey that the Irish were finally defeated and expelled from Wales in about AD 470.

Cunedda established himself at Aberffraw where he built a palace close to the site of the present day village. In doing so, he founded a dynasty which would rule North Wales for almost eight centuries and produce such notable leaders as Rhodri Mawr, Gruffydd ap Cynan, Owain Gwynedd, Llywelyn Fawr (Llywelyn the Great) and his grandson Llywelyn the Last, whose defeat by Edward I in 1282 brought a final end to Welsh independence.

The reign of Maelgwyn Gwynedd, a descendant of Cunedda's, saw the firm establishment of Christianity in Anglesey during the sixth century, with the founding of monasteries at Penmon and Holyhead by Saint Seiriol and Saint Cybi. Although he is said to have been a wicked ruler, the land on which these monasteries were built was granted by Maelgwyn. Perhaps he was looking for divine favour towards the end of his 'sinful' life.

The rule of the Welsh princes is unfortunately a rather sad period, being marked more by treachery than any great

The church at Penmon stands beside the ruins of the priory

advancement. The progress made by some of its greatest rulers was often destroyed by the infighting of their descendants. This was caused in part by the tradition of dividing a man's possessions equally between his sons following his death. The result was that at best his kingdom was much weakened, particularly if he had many sons, which was often the case. Siblings thus became rivals and frequently fought each other for their rightful share of their father's lands. Rivals were often eliminated or imprisoned. Prince Llywelyn for example, is said to have held one of his brothers in Castell Dolbadarn near Llanberis for over twenty years. Others made alliances with former enemies outside Wales in a desperate bid to gain their birthright.

This lack of unity—a trait first noted by the Romans—was quickly exploited by Saxons and Normans keen to expand their lands and influence. It also meant that when threatened, Wales as a nation was never able to defend itself with a united force.

During the early years of the ninth century a new menace presented itself; one that came to be feared throughout the British Isles and one that Anglesey was particularly vulnerable to— Viking raids. By this time the Vikings had formed colonies at Dublin and the Isle of Man and from there they launched attacks all along the Welsh coast. The monasteries at Holyhead and Penmon were attacked in 961 and 971 and the palace at Aberffraw was partially destroyed in 968. The Vikings left no settlements on Anglesey but a number of names remain as evidence of their passing; notably Priestholm (Puffin Island) and The Skerries off the northwestern tip of Anglesey.

The Norman conquest had little impact on Anglesey initially, although an early raid by the Earl of Chester in 1090 led to the building of a motte and bailey castle at Aberlleiniog near Beaumaris. This was soon destroyed by the powerful Gruffydd ap Cynan and the Normans made little real progress against the Welsh for the next 100 years.

When the threat of Viking raids ceased towards the end of the eleventh century, a period of prosperity followed and with an increase in population, a programme of church building began. It was at this time that churches were first built in stone and a number have survived, in part, from this period, notably Hen Chapel near Din Lligwy.

It was also during this time that deforestation of the interior of the island was finally achieved, releasing rich fertile land for agriculture and earning Anglesey the name 'Môn, Mam Cymru'—*Anglesey, Mother of Wales*. This referred to the vast quantities of grain which were grown here during the Middle Ages, sufficient it is said, to feed the whole of Wales.

During the wars of Llywelyn Fawr and his grandson Llywelyn

Beaumaris Castle

the Last, the importance of Anglesey's ability to feed Wales was realised and both King John and Edward I made attempts to take Anglesey, thus depriving Wales of its food supply. It was the loss of Anglesey which finally brought Llywelyn Fawr out of hiding in the highlands of Snowdonia to bargain with King John and ensured Edward's victory against Llywelyn the Last in 1282.

Following his conquest of Wales, Edward I embarked on a programme of castle building all along the North Wales coast, the ruins of which still stand. On Anglesey he built his last Welsh castle at Beaumaris in 1295 near the site of one of Llywelyn's courts at Llanfaes.

Mining spoil at Parys Mountain, near Amlwch

Wales was now subject to the English crown and the title 'Prince of Wales' reserved for the king's eldest son. The wars of independence were over, although Owain Glyndwr was to raise the Welsh banner briefly at the beginning of the fifteenth century.

Although Wales was never to see independence from the English crown again, it did produce one of the most influential ruling families ever to sit on the throne of England—the Tudors. The seat of this family was Plas Penmynydd in Anglesey and Henry Tudor's claim to the throne came through his descent from Owain Tudor and his rather mysterious marriage to Henry V's widow, Queen Catherine, in 1429.

The late sixteenth century saw an increased demand for

copper, required for the production of cannons and a host of household items. The Tudors were instrumental in restricting the import of foreign metal and the subsequent rise in the price of copper created great demand towards the end of the seventeenth century. The abandoned mines at Parys Mountain and the development of Amlwch as a port, are the result of the discovery and exploitation of one of the richest deposits of copper in the country.

The heyday of the industry was between 1760 and 1815 and the higher wages offered by the mining company took many

Ruins associated with the mines at Parys Mountain

workers off the land. Another industry from this period which we can still see remains of today, is that of milling. A number of old windmill towers remain as testimony to Anglesey's former corn production.

Anglesey's position in the Liverpool sea lane and its proximity to Ireland have produced a rich maritime history. By the seventeenth century, packet boats were regularly crossing to Ireland, providing a service which was to expand in the nineteenth century when Thomas Telford completed his London to Holyhead coach road (A5) and built the graceful suspension bridge over the Menai Strait in 1826.

Anglesey's rocky, treacherous coastline presented a constant hazard to shipping and there were literally hundreds of shipwrecks during the nineteenth century alone. The most famous wreck was that of the *'Royal Charter'*, which hit rocks and sank off Moelfre in 1859 with the loss of over 400 lives. The lighthouses which dot the coast today date mainly from this period although they are now all automated.

Today, tourism plays a key role in the island's economy and with road improvements on the mainland cutting the travelling time from Merseyside and Greater Manchester, Anglesey has become a popular venue for weekend breaks and second holidays. Away from the coast however, agriculture still dominates, although the emphasis is now on cattle and dairy farming, with little or no sign of its once famous corn fields.

Glossary of Welsh names

Aber	*river mouth*
Abaty	*abbey*
Afon	*river*
Bach	*little*
Bryn	*hill, eminence*
Cae	*field, enclosure*
Caer	*fort*
Canol	*middle*
Capel	*chapel*
Carn, Carnedd	*heap of stones*
Carreg	*crag or stone*
Castell	*castle or fortress*
Cefn	*ridge*
Clogwyn	*cliff*
Coch	*red*
Coed	*wood*
Cors	*bog or swamp*
Craig	*crag*
Croes/Groes	*cross*
Cwm	*coombe*
Dinas	*city, fortress*
Ddu	*black*
Dyffryn	*valley*
Eglwys	*church*
Eryri	*highland*
Esgair	*ridge*
Fach	*small*
Faes	*meadow*
Fawr	*large*
Felin	*mill*
Ffordd	*road*
Ffynnon	*well or fountain*
Foel	*bare hill*
Gaer	*camp*
Galt	*slope*
Glas	*blue-green*
Glyn	*deep valley*
Goch	*red*
Gors	*swamp*
Grach	*scabby*
Gwyn	*white*
Hafod	*summer dwelling*
Hen	*old*
Isaf	*lower*
Llan	*church*
Llyn	*lake*
Llys	*hall or court*
Lon	*lane*
Maen	*stone*
Maes	*field or meadow*
Mawr	*large*
Moel	*rounded hill*
Mor	*sea*
Morfa	*flat seashore, sea fen*
Mynach	*monk*
Mynydd	*mountain*
Newydd	*new*
Ogof	*cave*
Pant	*hollow*
Parc	*park*
Pen	*head or point*
Penrhyn	*promontory*
Pentre	*village*
Pistyll	*waterfall*
Plas	*house*
Pont	*bridge*
Porth	*port*
Pwll	*pool*
Rhos	*moorland*
Rhyd	*ford*
Sarn	*causeway*
Tomen	*mound*
Traeth	*beach, sandy shore*
Tref	*town*
Trwyn	*peninsula*
Twll	*cavern*
Twr	*tower*
Ty	*house*
Tyddyn	*farmstead*
Uchaf	*upper*
Waun	*moorland*
Wen	*white*
Wern/Gwern	*alder swamp*
Y, Yr	*the*
Yn	*in*
Ynys	*island*

Beaumaris

Distance: *5¹/₂ miles*

A varied route exploring the island's eastern tip. The limestone walls, lush green fields and hedgerows are unusual for Anglesey and are confined to this sheltered corner of the island.

Start: There are numerous places where cars can be parked in Beaumaris, along with two large long stay car parks. Begin the walk outside the castle entrance opposite the 'White Lion Hotel'. A section of this walk is affected by the state of the tide. Consult tide tables before starting (see note below).
Grid ref: 608 760 (Landranger 114, Explorer 263)

The walk

1. With the castle entrance behind you turn left along the road passing a play area on your left. About 80 yards after traffic lights, bear right down a one-way road. Follow the short road to the waters' edge where it turns sharp right. Turn left through a kissing gate here and out into a field. Go ahead on the path which runs close to the crumbling cliff edge overlooking the Menai Strait.

This path gives fine views out over the Menai Strait to the mainland where the rounded slopes of the Carneddau rise behind the coastal towns of Llanfairfechan and Penmaenmawr. To the east the weathered limestone headlands of Penmon and the Great Orme reach out into the Irish Sea.

The path now drops to the road. Walk along the road until it turns away from the shore at the end of the bay. Drop down onto the beach and follow the shore for about 1 mile.

Warning: High tides cover much of this beach and reach right

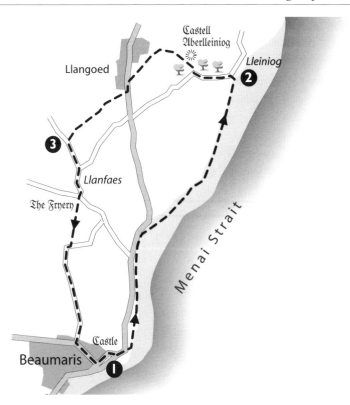

up to the crumbling cliffs near Lleiniog—the shore is accessible apart from 1 hour either side of high tide. You will need about 30-40 minutes to complete this section, if the tide is low or falling there should be no problem.

As you approach Lleiniog there are some interesting formations in the cliffs which clearly show the layering and composition of the glacial drift which covers much of the island.

2. At Lleiniog bear left by the river which flows across the beach and at the road turn left. After about ¼ mile look for a narrow track on the right among the trees. Turn right here and follow the track beside the stream to join the concrete access road to the treatment works on you right.

The ruins visible in the trees to the right of the path are those of

Beaumaris

Castell Aberlleiniog, a Norman motte and bailey fort built by the Earl of Chester in 1090. The original structure was destroyed just three years later by Gruffydd ap Cynan causing the Normans to abandon Anglesey for the next 100 years. The present stone ruins are thought to date from the medieval period.

Walk up the road and turn left at the first house keeping to the left to join an enclosed footpath. At a T junction and kissing gate, keep left and walk beside gardens on the right eventually joining the road at Llangoed. Turn left here and after about 100 yards cross over and turn right onto a well used field path. After a stile enter a caravan and camping site. Walk through the site passing the toilet block and partway through an area of caravans, a yellow arrow on a post directs you half-right to a second arrow which indicates a right turn to a stile in the hedge behind one of the caravans. Walk half-left across two fields aiming for the Bulkeley Memorial high on the skyline.

3. Turn left into a narrow lane and continue to Llanfaes. The little church here is all that now recalls the site of Llanfaes, once the major trading centre of the island.

It was here that Llywelyn the Great had a court and founded the Franciscan Abbey which was to become the burial place of his wife Princess Joan, the daughter of King John in 1239. Part of her stone coffin can be seen in the doorway of St Mary's Church in Beaumaris but nothing remains of the abbey.

When Edward I decided on this location for his final Welsh castle along with the adjoining borough of Beaumaris, the inhabitants of Llanfaes were evicted and moved to a 'new borough' in the exposed southwest tip of the island. Today this village is known as Newborough.

Where the lane bends sharp right, turn left (ignore first left to the church) and look for a small gate and fingerpost beside the large gate posts to the Friary. Go through the gate and follow the right of way directly across the following field and golf course, rising to where stone steps lead into a quiet lane. Turn right here and follow the lane left around the bend and back to Beaumaris.

Beaumaris came into existence as a borough in 1296 with the building of Edward I's castle. The name is thought to be derived from the old French 'beau mareys' meaning the 'beautiful marsh'. The land on which the castle and the town stands originally lay on the edge of the Menai Strait and ships could dock alongside the castle walls. Much of the present town was thus built on reclaimed marsh land and its setting could certainly be described as beautiful—backed by the rich farmland of Anglesey with wide views across the Menai Strait to the mountains of Snowdonia.

Beaumaris was the last of Edward's Welsh castles to be built and although its construction covered a period of 30 years, it was never completed. It did however, see action in the Glyndwr rising of the early fifteenth century and the Civil War in the 1640s.

The castle is unique in being the only one of the ring of fortresses with which Edward encircled North Wales to be built on flat low-lying ground. This however, enabled its architect, Master James of St George, to produce a symmetric design not possible at any other Welsh sites. For this same reason the castle is sometimes disappointing to the visitor. It has none of the commanding skylines or dominating presence of Caernarfon, Harlech or Conwy. Its strength comes from its concentric defences. A moat fed by tidal water encircled the outer wall, which in turn presented a line of defence which, if breached left attackers little better off. The walls of the inner ward are even higher and the towers—positioned forward from the wall line—gave defenders a clear view along the outside of the walls.

The use of gunpowder in the late Middle Ages left castles defenceless and most, including Beaumaris, fell into ruins. Interest was only revived when visitors began to come to North Wales towards the end of the eighteenth century and during the Victorian period.

In 1925 Sir Richard Williams-Bulkely gave the castle to the Commissioners of Works for preservation as an ancient monument. Renovation work followed and resulted in the clearing out and re-establishment of the moat on the west side and the removal of vast undergrowth which can be seen clothing the walls in many early drawings. Today the castle is one of the most popular attractions on the island.

Red Wharf Bay

Distance: *4 or 5¹/₄ miles*

A mixed undulating walk over tidal sands, marsh and through woodlands on an unfrequented section of the coast. Footpaths are generally good although care should be exercised with the tides (see note below).

Start: There is free car parking available on the shore at the southern end of Red Wharf Bay. This can be reached by taking the narrow lane (Lôn y Traeth) which runs down to the bay from the B5109 at Pentraeth.

Like the previous route care with the tides must be exercised with this walk. High tides cover all the sand and much of the marsh around the edges of the bay making walking difficult and even dangerous at certain times. Cars left on the beach may also be at risk from high tides. Consult tide tables and time the walk to coincide with a falling tide to be safe.
Grid ref. 535 798 (Landranger 114, Explorer 263).

The walk

1. Walk east (to the right when looking out to sea) along the edge of the sand and marsh for about 1¹/₄ miles.

Just beyond a small wooden beach house a lane reaches down onto the sand. Here you have a choice—either turn right up the lane and then right again into the first access road on the right (continue from point **2.**) or continue along the beach (1 mile) for a longer round.

For the longer walk, keep ahead on a signed footpath which follows the top of a sea wall.

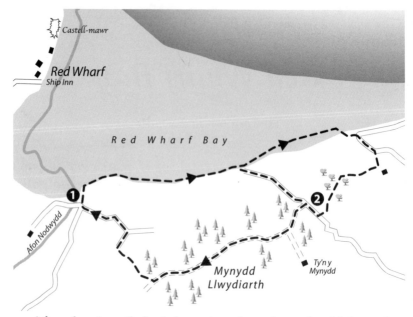

After about a mile look for a signed sandy track which reaches down onto the beach on the right (large aerial on hillside above). This soon joins a road which curves in from the left. Keep straight ahead here following the lane for about 250 yards to a signed footpath and ladder stile on the right. Follow the path to a gate and rise to a T junction with a more prominent track. Turn right here and contour the hillside to enter a small wood after the second field (stone farm building on left). Follow the path through the wood and enter a field again by a metal kissing gate. Keep to the right-hand field edge and enter a second larger wood. Shortly the path forks, keep right here and remain on the prominent path for about 300 yards.

Although woodland clothed much of Anglesey until the early Middle Ages, trees are a rare sight in many parts of the island today, especially in the exposed north and west. Here on the east however, woods are more numerous giving the landscape a completely different look. The wooded hillsides which surround Red Wharf Bay make it one of the prettiest bays on the island.

Walking along the beach at the start of the walk

The path emerges from the woods by houses; turn left up the access road. At the lane turn right.

2. After about 150 yards turn into an access road on the left (this will be on the right if you are coming up from the beach on the shorter walk). Walk up the road passing houses on either side. After the last house the track enters the forest and shortly a junction is reached with a track on the left. Ignore this continuing straight ahead on the prominent forest road. Ignore a signed path and forest road on the right after about 400 yards and continue ahead for another ³/₄ mile.

At a large area of felled trees, stay on the prominent forest road ignoring a path which forks left into the clearing.

This clearing allows a fine view over Anglesey's flat interior set against a background of Snowdonia's highest peaks and the shapely hills of the Lleyn peninsula.

About 400 yards further on a broad forest road joins from the left. Ignore this, instead, follow the track as it bears right and drops. At the bottom of the dip look for a yellow arrow on a low post directing you right onto a narrow but obvious footpath (the forest road begins to rise again beyond this). Follow the path through the trees and leave the woods by a stile. Ignore a crossing path and walk directly down the hillside through an area of rough heather and gorse with a wide view of the bay, to enter an access track. Turn right down the track and at the first sharp bend go through a small gate straight ahead and turn right. Keep descending and at a T junction with a white cottage to the left, turn left. Follow the tarmac road back to the car park to complete the walk.

Red Wharf

Distance: *5 miles*

A gentle walk along the western edge of Red Wharf Bay to the resort of Benllech, with a return by quiet inland lanes and footpaths. The area is well walked and most of the footpaths are excellent.

Start: There is a small car park beside the 'Ship Inn' situated at the end of the lane leading down to the beach at Red Wharf from the A5025.
Grid ref. 529 810 (Landranger 114, Explorer 263).

The walk

1. From the 'Ship Inn' walk north (to the right when facing the pub) along the road parallel to the beach.

From here you have a fine view across the tidal sands of Red Wharf Bay, arguably one of the most attractive bays on Anglesey. Geologically it is the eastern counterpart of the Cefni estuary, with just five miles separating the two. Unlike Red Wharf Bay, the sands of Afon Cefni have been extensively reclaimed so that the estuary today is a fraction of its former size. Originally Red Wharf Bay and Afon Cefni almost divided Anglesey into two separate islands.

One of the most attractive features of Red Wharf Bay and one which is quite rare on Anglesey is its backdrop of hills. The wooded Mynydd Llwydiarth and the limestone plateau of Bwrdd Arthur, both rising to over 500 feet, stand guard over the southern arm of the bay and isolate its eastern shore. Woods are also a feature of this locality. Elsewhere on the island deforestation since the Middle Ages has left the landscape bare, while grazing and winter gales have made the regeneration of woodland almost impossible.

Ignoring the drive to 'Traeth Coch Sailing Club' continue to the end of the driveway where there is a large house. Bear left here almost back on yourself onto a rising path. The path turns right just before a caravan site and runs close to the huge limestone block known as

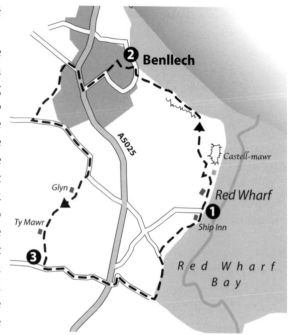

Castell Mawr on the right. Do not go through the gate on the right at the end of the path, instead turn left onto a path leading into a caravan site and at the site access road turn right. After about 20 yards bear left onto the signed coastal path. Follow this path through the trees parallel to the site road. Where the path forks, bear right as signed and stay on the obvious path passing a tower behind the clubhouse. Just before the beach turn left onto a surfaced footpath. This path weaves in and out of the trees close to cliffs on the left to emerge above the beach. Rise to join a concrete path and follow this to the road. Turn right down the hill to Benllech.

Benllech has long been one of the most popular resorts on the island and a hot summer's day will find the beach and sea front packed with visitors. An assortment of cafes and gift shops selling ice cream and other seaside paraphernalia decorate the short sea front and give the place its 'traditional seaside' atmosphere.

The centre of the village lies away from the sea front and straddles the A5025 indicating that it did not originate as a fishing village like nearby Moelfre. Development spread down the hillside towards the beach as its popularity grew in the early twentieth century. The name Benllech means 'head of the rock' from the words 'pen' and 'llech', —most likely a reference to the nearby sea cliffs.

2. Walk past the 'Wendon Café' and turn left into the car park crossing diagonally to where a flight of wooden steps by the WC block rise to a footpath. Turn right here and where the path forks higher up, keep left eventually reaching a metal kissing gate.

Go through the gate and turn left up the road ('Bay View Road'). At the main road (A5025) turn right and just before the

Boats on the shore at Red Wharf where the walk starts

'Plas Glanrafon Hotel' bear left into 'Lôn Pant y Cudyn'. Almost immediately, turn left through a kissing gate onto a signed footpath beside a stream. This eventually runs into fields by another kissing gate. Follow the well used footpath straight ahead through several fields marked by stiles to a lane. Turn left here and follow the lane for just under ½ mile.

Immediately after a large wood on the right, turn right down the drive to 'Glyn'. Pass through the farm and at the top of the rise where the road bends left; bear right into a green lane. Where the green lane turns to the right, keep straight ahead along a short enclosed track which leads into a field. Keep to the left-hand field edge to a kissing gate in the far corner adjacent to a house ('Ty Mawr'). Walk straight ahead with the house on your right and look for a small gate beside a large field gate, also on the right, after about 100 yards. Go through the gate and turn left down the drive.

At the first bend go through a gate straight ahead. Follow the path with an over grown bank to the right to emerge in a small field. Go ahead through the field to a ladder stile which leads into playing fields. Bear left around the edge of the field to a second stile in the opposite corner. Cross a small field now to enter a lane by the local primary school.

3. Turn left and follow the lane to the A5025. Cross over and walk down a narrow path opposite which joins a descending lane. Turn left down the lane and follow it to the shore.

Turn left along the marshy and sometimes muddy path which runs along the high tide mark. (In exceptionally high tides this may be submerged.) At a group of houses bear left up a tarmac road and after about 100 yards look for the signed coastal footpath on the right (kissing gate). Walk across a small field to a second kissing gate which leads onto an enclosed footpath. Follow this footpath to emerge in Red Wharf beside the 'Ship Inn' to complete the walk.

Beaumaris (route 1)

Red Wharf (route 3)

Moelfre (route 4)

Porth Eilian and Point Lynas (route 5)

Disused brickworks at Porth Wen (route 6)

Ynys y Fydlyn (route 9)

The White Ladies beacons, Carmel Head (route 9)

Elen's Tower, South Stack (route 11)

Looking across Holyhead Bay (route 11)

South Stack Lighthouse from Penrhyn Mawr (route 12)

South Stack Lighthouse from Penrhyn Mawr (route 12)

Cymyran (route 13)

Traeth Crigyll, Rhosneigr (route 14)

Wild orchids are seen frequently along the coast

Mid summer sunset near Red Wharf Bay

Yr Eifl (The Rivals) from Newborough Warren (route 15)

Moelfre

Distance: *4¹/₄ miles*

An easy walk along a popular section of coastal path and quiet country lanes. Footpaths are excellent throughout.

The walk has the option to visit the historic sites of Din Lligwy Iron Age village, the Lligwy Burial Chamber and the rocks on which the 'Royal Charter' was wrecked in 1859.

Start: Begin the walk from the large beach car park at Traeth Bychan, situated at the end of a lane off the A5025 partway between Moelfre and Benllech.
Grid ref: 513 850 (Landranger 114, Explorer 263).

The walk

1. From the car park walk down towards the beach and just beyond the beach café bear left through a small gate indicated by the coastal path sign. Keep to the right up the field. Go through a kissing gate and follow the field boundary on your left through two fields to join an enclosed path. The path eventually enters a farmyard at 'Nant Bychan'. Bear right along the farm access road.

Keep a look out for the coastal path sign on the right which directs you down to the little shingle bay at Porth yr Aber. Turn right here and at the cove bear left across the flat rocks to join the coastal path again. Continue to Moelfre. At the road turn right down the hill to the centre of the village.

Moelfre is one the most attractive coastal villages on the island. The tiny sea front and pebble beach is south facing and protected by a headland to the north. The prevailing westerlies, even on a blustery day, have largely exhausted themselves by the time they reach this part of the island and visitors can often enjoy warm spring or autumn sunshine here. The small size of the village does mean that it will be busy in the holiday season and there is little room for parking.

Just before the beach you will pass a large metal anchor on the right. This was taken from the wreck of the 'Hindlea' which hit rocks nearby on 27 October 1959, almost 100 years to the day since one of the most famous shipping disasters of the nineteenth century occurred in the same location—the sinking of the 'Royal Charter'. The 'Hindlea' was a Cardiff vessel and radioed for assistance when she could no longer make progress against gale force winds and mountainous waves. The Moelfre lifeboat was launched and managed to rescue eight crew members. For this brilliant rescue the lifeboat crew, led by Coxswain Evans received medals for their bravery. Within twenty minutes of the rescue the 'Hindlea' was smashed to pieces on the nearby sea cliffs.

2. Follow the road around the little cove and as it rises and bends left away from the sea, turn right onto a paved footpath which overlooks the bay. Pass the Seawatch Centre and Moelfre Lifeboat

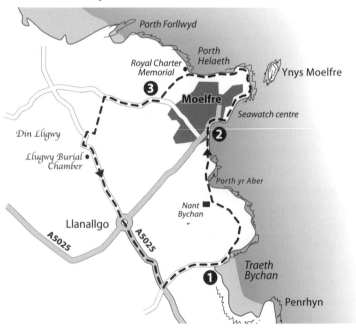

Moelfre

Station and continue to the little shingle beach opposite the islet of Ynys Moelfre with its colony of sea birds. Turn left here across a small shingle beach. At the end of the shingle by a row of low cottages on the left, join the coastal path ahead.

Where the path enters a small caravan site near Porth Helaeth, keep left ignoring the continuation of the coastal path (unless you wish to visit the Royal Charter Memorial a few hundred yards across the bay) and follow the access road out of the site. At a T Junction turn right and shortly reach the road.

The wreck of the 'Royal Charter' was one of the worst shipping disasters of the nineteenth century and shocked the entire nation. The severe storm which lashed Britain for two days on the 25th and 26th October 1859 resulted in the loss of around 222 vessels in all. Of these over 100 were wrecked around the Welsh coast and the casualty list came to over 800 lives lost. Over half of these perished on the 'Royal Charter'.

The ship was on the home run from Australia to Liverpool and many of her passengers were returning from the Australian gold fields with their hard earned money. When the ship ran aground many individuals tried to swim ashore with their gold tied around their waists or in money belts but were dragged to their deaths by the money's weight. No women or children survived the sinking.

At the time it seemed inconceivable that such a well equipped ship of 2719 tons could come to grief less than two hours from her home port of Liverpool. In the following weeks many well known individuals came to visit Moelfre to see the bay where the ship went down. Among these was the writer Charles Dickens. He was deeply moved by the disaster and its aftermath and commented on the work carried out by the vicar of Llanallgo where most of the victims were buried. He answered over 1,000 letters of inquiry in ten weeks. Dickens wrote: 'The Vicar worked alone for hours solemnly surrounded by eyes that could not see him and lips that could not speak to him, patiently examining the tattered clothing, cutting off buttons, hair, marks from linen, anything that might lead to subsequent identification.'

3. Turn right along the road and after about ¼ mile, just beyond the drive to 'Aber Farm', turn left through two kissing gates past a small quarry and into fields. Keep to field edges and in the far corner of the second field, turn right over the stile. Keep left along the field edge to enter a quiet lane.

Turn left along the lane and after the first bend look for the massive capstone of the Lligwy Burial Chamber on the right.

At first the chamber seems rather squat, but a closer inspection will reveal that almost two thirds lie below ground level making use of a natural fissure in the rock. The massive capstone, estimated to weigh over 25 tons, is supported on small upright stones. The monument is thought to date from the late Neolithic period.

Continue along the lane to the roundabout at Llanallgo. Go straight ahead here and follow the main road for about ½ mile to the crossroads. Turn left down the lane back to the beach car park to complete the walk.

Porth Amlwch

Distance: *4½ miles*

An easy gentle walk centred on the once busy port of Amlwch.
Field paths, lanes and a quiet stretch of coastline.

Start: There is a small car park in 'Quay Street' near the 'Liverpool Arms' and the 'Adelphi Vaults' in Porth Amlwch.
Grid ref: 449 931 (Landranger 114, Explorer 263).

The walk

1. Walk past the 'Adelphi Vaults', turn left at the T junction (opposite the 'Liverpool Arms') and take the first road on the right ('Broc yr Odyn'). At the end of this short access road there is a kissing gate (ignore this) and immediately to the left an enclosed footpath leads to a ladder stile. Take this path and enter a scrubby field after the stile. Keep to the right-hand edge and look for a kissing gate after high stone walling. Turn right through the gate and cut directly through an area of gorse. Keep with the hedge on the right.

In the field corner with kissing gates ahead and to the right, turn left (before the kissing gates) and follow the footpath to a kissing gate in the opposite corner. Turn left for a couple of yards, then right along an access road and walk towards a large house on the left. Walk past the house joining a green lane to a stile on the left at the end of the lane.

Walk straight ahead for about 75 yards then turn right down the bank and pass through a gap in the stone wall on your right. Bear half-left and walk directly across the following large field. The second half of this field is composed of flat rock outcrops and the ladder stile in the far fence can not be seen from here, so aim just to the left of aerials on the skyline.

The ladder stile leads onto a path through gorse which is soon enclosed by low stone walls and rises towards a small farm. Immediately before the farm stone steps in the wall on the left take you into a field. Walk across the field aiming to the right of a large house. Enter the lane here, turn left and opposite the second driveway to the house 'Bryn Eilian', turn right through a kissing gate. Follow the path beside a stone wall, then through a small field keeping right down stone steps to the lane again. Turn left along the lane and continue to Llaneilian church.

Pass the church and take the first lane on the left. Follow this down to the little cove of Porth Eilian.

2. Immediately before the cove turn left onto the signed coastal path. This is well walked and easily followed.

After the inlet of Porthyrychen, look for a much smaller inlet where a stream crosses the path. To your left a large rock lies beside the stream and to the left of this, a second rock has a spring bubbling from beneath it. This is known locally as Ffynnon Eilian.

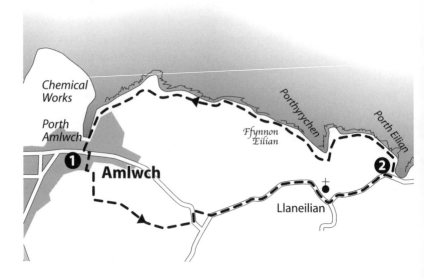

Ffynnon Eilian is said to be the well of St Eilian who founded the nearby church in the sixth century on land granted to him by Caswallon, the king of Gwynedd at that time. The well is said to have been used as a cursing well, possibly connected to a story in which Eilian is said to have struck the king blind for some misdemeanour. The land on which Eilian founded his church is said to have been given to him in gratitude for the king's regained sight. Remnants of a dry-stone wall enclosing the well can still be seen at the foot of the large rock from which the water flows.

From Ffynnon Eilian continue along the coastal path for about ^{1}/2 mile.

At a larger inlet with a small house beyond, go through a kissing gate and aim for a second kissing gate to the left of the house. From here a short walk leads to the road. Follow the road back to Porth Amlwch.

Porth Amlwch owes its existence to the rich copper reserves to be found at nearby Parys Mountain. The Romans are thought to have mined copper here but it is almost certain that such rich reserves would not have gone unnoticed in an area so rich in prehistoric remains. After the Romans there seems to have been little interest in the copper here until a sharp rise in prices began in the late seventeenth century. The reasons behind this were an increased use of the metal in the production of guns and as protection for the hulls of wooden ships. In addition to this, the Tudor monarchy favoured the use of the home market and brought policies into force which resisted the use of imports.

By the beginning of the eighteenth century, all the conditions were right for a boom in the copper industry and Parys Mountain was one of the richest reserves in the country. The peak came in the latter half of the eighteenth century when two local entrepreneurs, Sir Nicholas Bayly and Rev Edward Hughes developed the mines to their greatest extent. By this time some 1,500 people were employed and the mining companies were even minting their own coins. Local agriculture must have suffered badly as higher wages offered by the mining companies took workers off the land.

Porth Amlwch

The condition of roads in North Wales was still poor at this time so the obvious method of transportation was by sea. The Port of Amlwch was born. Smelting industries were also developed here and as production from the mines reached 44,000 tons per year the town grew from a small village into a prosperous market town.

With so much hanging on the price of copper things were always going to be fickle and the turn of the nineteenth century saw the beginning of a decline in the fortunes of the town. One of the main factors in this seems to have been the end of the Napoleonic wars and the lifting of restrictions on foreign imports. Throughout the early nineteenth century the price of copper continued to fall and the mines declined. They were no longer of any significance after the 1850s.

Bull Bay

Distance: 4¹/₄ miles

A moderate gentle walk on a quiet section of the coast; only in the approach to Bull Bay are you likely to meet other walkers. There are some interesting industrial remains at Porth Wen but they are in a derelict condition and are best viewed from a distance.

Start: Take the A 5025 west from Amlwch and pass through Bull Bay. After about 2 miles, turn right into a narrow lane. After about ¹/₂ mile and just beyond a farm on the left, park on the verge beside two signed footpaths.
Grid ref. 398 943 (Landranger 114, Explorer 262).

The walk

1. Take the first of the two signed footpaths (when approaching from the A5025). Go ahead through the first field beside the wall to a kissing gate. Bear half-right through the following field to a second kissing gate. Go ahead through the field in the direction of a stone farmhouse across the bay. Pass through an area of gorse bearing left down the bank. Turn right passing a squat waymarker post and cross a footbridge over a stream. Go through a kissing gate and walk around the left-hand edge of the field and towards the stone farmhouse seen earlier.

Pass the farmhouse on the right and follow the access road. Where this bends right keep ahead on the signed coastal path. Walk along a short grass track which soon opens out into a field.

2. Keep left along the field edge overlooking the bay.

Porth Wen

Porth Wen is a wide unfriendly bay lined with steep cliffs and impressive rock scenery. With only a small beach to absorb the impact of winter storms, the slaty rock has weathered into a series of jagged narrow inlets which cut in towards the path.

On the far side of the bay you will see the abandoned remains of Porth Wen Brickworks with its tall chimneys and distinctive beehive shaped kilns. This enterprise used quartzite from nearby Craig Wen to make silica bricks for use in the steel industry. These were exported by boat from the little quay which can be seen adjacent to the works.

The existence of quartzite here probably gave the bay its name: Porth Wen means 'white port' and Craig Wen, from where the crystal was taken, means 'white crag' or 'white rock'.

Between here and Bull Bay the coastal path is well used and easily followed along the low cliffs and easy angled coastal slope.

3. As you approach Bull Bay there are two kissing gates adjacent to one another. Go through the gate ahead which takes you on to a footpath around the little headland which encloses the cove.

At a tarmac access road by a house, go ahead along the road and in about 50 yards turn left through a kissing gate. Follow the narrow footpath with gardens to the right (bay to the left) to the road by the 'Bull Bay Hotel' on the right.

Out to the east of Bull Bay you will be able to see the little rock of East Mouse or Ynys Amlwch. It was on this rock that the huge steam ship 'Dakota', one of the largest steamships to be wrecked on the Anglesey coast, ran aground and became a total wreck in 1877. The 'Dakota' was almost 400 feet long and built for speed to cover the transatlantic crossing—a feature which led to her downfall. The ship was outward bound for New York and just a few hours into the journey when the order was given to turn away from the coast. For reasons which have never been fully explained, the ship turned the wrong way and headed straight for the treacherous northern coast of the island. By the time the error was realised it was too late: the ship hit the rock and became a total wreck. All 218 passengers were rescued by the Bull Bay lifeboat but the reason for the helmsman's error remains a mystery.

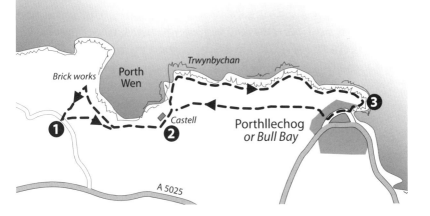

Take the road opposite and walk up the rising lane. Adjacent to a row of houses on the right almost at the top of the rise, turn right down the 'Private Road to Bryn Arthur and St Eleth'. Just before the house ('Bryn Arthur'), where the road bends right, bear left onto a signed footpath which leads into fields. Bear left through the field to a stile beside a metal gate which leads onto a track. Turn right along the track and look for an iron kissing gate in the wall on the left just before a farmhouse ('Ty Gwyn'). Cut directly through two small fields to join a second access road with a house to the right. The right of way continues opposite, where a gate leads into fields once more. Keep right around the field edge and in the top corner of the field go through a gap in the ruined wall.

Turn half-left now up towards a small stone pillar and go through a gap in the wall. Follow the crest of a rocky rounded rib ahead until the wide bay of Porth Wen comes into view. As you start to descend look for a kissing gate in the corner of a field on the left. Go through the kissing gate and keep ahead along the field edge beside the wall. Stay beside the wall as it bends leftwards to eventually join the short grass track used earlier (by the stone farmhouse).

Retrace your steps past the farmhouse and through the following fields crossing the footbridge over the stream. In the next field follow the coastal path around the right-hand field edge immediately backing the bay. Cross the stile in the top corner of the field and go ahead to a second stile. Cross this and go ahead again to a T junction with a broad path/track. Turn left and follow this path back to the lane to complete the walk.

Cemaes Bay

Distance: *3¹/₂ miles*

A short easy coastal walk on good footpaths centred on Cemaes, the most northerly village in Wales.

Start: There is a free car park adjacent to Wylfa Power Station. This is situated at the end of the lane which runs north to Wylfa Head (turn right immediately before the gates to Wylfa Power Station and Visitor Centre). The lane leaves the A5025 at a point between Tregele and Cemaes Bay and is signed to 'Wylfa Power Station and Visitor Centre'.
Grid ref. 356 938 (Landranger 114, Explorer 262).

The walk

1. Walk out of the car park and turn right through a kissing gate adjacent to the large gates and pillars which were once part of Wylfa Hall. Ignore the obvious path which curves left from here and the path straight ahead, instead, bear half-right on a footpath which passes a walled enclosure on the right and leads into a large open field. Take a direct line across the field to a second kissing gate in the far wall. Walk directly across the following field for about 150 yards aiming just to the left of a large house on the skyline. A kissing gate on the left leads onto the coast edge overlooking Porth Wylfa. Go through the gate and follow the path above the bay. After about 250 yards look for a kissing gate and footpath on the right which leads up towards a large house.

The right of way keeps to the right-hand field edge, passes over the access road immediately in front of the house, then continues to enter a green lane with large stone gateposts. Turn right, then immediately left through a kissing gate and keep left along the field edge. In the bottom of the second field, bear right to a kissing gate which leads onto an enclosed footpath. At a T junction turn left and follow a well made footpath to join the road in Cemaes.

A right turn here will take you into the centre of Cemaes where there are shops and pubs and there is a fine beach with safe bathing.

Like most villages on the Welsh coast, Cemaes originated as a fishing village although it does have the distinction of being Wales' most northerly settlement. Prior to the great road improvements of the nineteenth century, poor inland communication links meant that travel by sea was Cemaes only reliable link with the outside world. This led to the development of a small harbour which by the early nineteenth century consisted of a stone pier behind which the fishing boats sheltered from the frequent winter storms. In 1828 a particularly violent storm destroyed part of this structure and a new one was designed by Ishmael Jones, a local entrepreneur. This was complete by 1835 and a small ship building industry developed with vessels from 100 to 400 tons being built here.

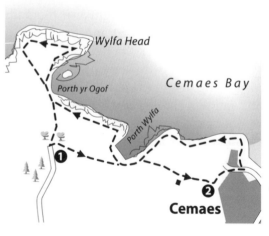

Ships from Cemaes traded in coal, limestone, corn, marble, lime and ochre. An indication of Cemaes commercial links with England at this time can be seen in the fact that many public buildings in Liverpool are built from limestone and marble exported from Cemaes. The harbour

Cemaes

also benefited from the success of the nearby copper mines at Parys Mountain.

Cemaes sea-trade began to decline in the mid-nineteenth century with the introduction of the railways and the improvement of the road system on the mainland. Today the village markets itself as a holiday resort. There is a fine, safe beach and the surrounding coastal scenery is among the finest on the island. It is also a popular location for fishing, sailing and bird watching.

2. To continue the walk, cross the road (or return from the village centre) and take the signed footpath opposite. Walk up a steep tarmac access road and where this levels turn right onto a narrow signed (coastal path) footpath with a stone cottage immediately to the right. At an access road turn left and follow this to a kissing gate on the right where the road bends left. This is a permissive footpath (closed to the public on the 25 November each year) which gives the public access to the coast edge.

Beyond the houses the path bends left to meet the access road to Park Lodge (the large house passed earlier). Follow the signed footpath to the right here, turning sharp right after 20 yards to continue on the permissive path along the coast edge (the right of way goes directly up the field from here).

There is a fine view back to the village from the top of the rise and in clear conditions the peaks of Snowdonia can be seen on the skyline.

As you round the bay into Porth Wylfa go through a kissing gate and cross the field to a second kissing gate. You can cut the walk short here by going straight ahead back to the car park, alternatively, turn right along the field edge. Soon you are overlooking the sea again on a faint permissive path which takes you to Porth yr Ogof where there is a small island with a cave and the remains of a slipway.

Shortly after this the path takes you through a gateway onto the open land at Wylfa Head.

A plaque on the wall here records that the land at Wylfa Head was given to the parishioners of Llanbadrig in 1969 by the Central Electricity Board to celebrate the investiture of Prince Charles.

Immediately after the gateway turn right onto a path which follows the coast with views out to the right across the bay to Cemaes. Follow the path to the ruined lookout on the northern tip of the head. Continue around the head with the huge bulk of Wylfa Power Station in front of you.

There is no specific path or right of way as the head is open access land so you can pick your own route, but you should trend left soon heading for the gateway used earlier. Go through the gateway and continue ahead to pass through a gap in the wall. Bear half-right here on a path across the field to a kissing gate which leads through a picnic area and the woods beyond to the car park to complete the walk.

Wylfa & Cemlyn Bay

Distance: *6 miles*

A moderate walk almost entirely on the level, starting in the woods at Wylfa Power Station and visiting the unusual beach and tidal lagoon at Cemlyn. A return is made along quiet lanes and field paths.

Note: *The outlet from the lagoon at Cemlyn Bay can not be crossed at certain points of the tide. Due to the way the lagoon fills and empties through this outlet, access is better after low tide. A crossing can usually be made up to 5 hours after low tide, but at times may not be possible for up to 3 hours after high tide.*

Start: As for the previous route.
Grid ref. 356 938 (Landranger 114, Explorer 262).

The walk

1. Almost opposite the car park entrance there is a stile into woods. Cross this stile and follow the path through the trees. At a T junction turn left, make a short rise, then descend a zig-zag path. Pass beneath a large pylon keeping ahead and ignoring a path to the left. The path continues between gorse before bearing right away from the pylons and into trees again. At a clearing, turn left to join the main access road to the power station. Almost opposite the visitor centre turn right onto a signed footpath which leads to a field gate. Follow the track beyond the gate with a high wall to the right. At the end of the track a kissing gate takes you into fields. Keep left here along the field edge with views of the power station to the right.

As you approach farm buildings, turn left through a kissing

gate in the field corner and look for a second kissing gate on the right after a few yards. Walk directly across the field now, ignoring a ladder stile on the right. Aim for the right-hand edge of a small wood where you should drop down the bank to a small stone stile. This takes you into a tiny cove with the gardens of 'Cestyll' to the left and a small stone footbridge over the stream. Pass the old mill on your left, and follow the coastline onto the headland beyond.

To the right there is a good view of Wylfa Power Station dominating the surrounding landscape and looking quite out of place in such an otherwise remote location. The power station has been in operation since 1971. Its two reactors produce 23 million kilowatt hours of electricity— enough to supply large cities such as Liverpool and Manchester.

The path stays outside walled fields on the left passing the islet of Cerrig Brith before curving left into Cemlyn Bay. Continue to the beach where there is a car park.

The unusual formation of this beach has been caused by centuries of onshore winds, depositing stones and shingle across the

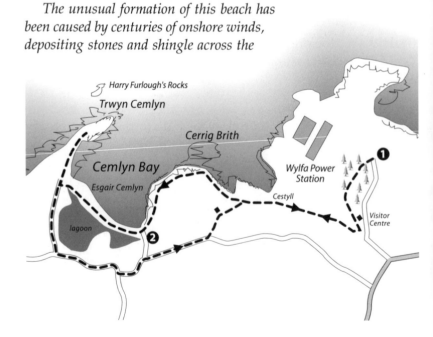

Cemlyn Bay

mouth of the bay to form a ridge (esgair). This has created a brackish lagoon on the landward side fed by fresh water and inundated by the sea only on the highest tides. Water level in the lagoon is maintained by a weir at the far end of the beach built in the 1930s and repaired in 1978.

The lagoon was managed as a private wildlife refuge for 40 years until the National Trust bought it with funds from Enterprise Neptune in 1971. It is now leased by North Wales Wildlife Trust who maintain it as a nature reserve. Unsurprisingly, the pool is a haven for wildlife and supports large numbers of grey mullet along with a variety of wildfowl including mallard, shelduck, redshank, oystercatcher, red-breasted merganser, coot, little grebe and tufted duck.

Of particular note is the tern colony, which is one of the largest in Britain and returns here each spring to breed. The reserve provides a unique opportunity to view a tern colony at such close quarters, although you are requested to follow the viewing instructions so as not to disturb birds during the breeding season. Please do not walk along the grass bank by the pool between April and July when the birds are nesting.

2. Continue ahead along the beach (Esgair Cemlyn) and at the far end cross the outlet stream from the lagoon (during high tides this may not be possible—see note at the beginning of the chapter). Turn right now and walk over flat rocks beside a high wall and deserted farmhouse on the left to a track. A right turn here will take you onto the National Trust land at Trwyn Cemlyn where a wide view of the bay can be enjoyed (return to this point to continue the walk). Alternatively, turn left and walk down the lane.

A stone memorial on the path to Trwyn Penrhyn commemorates the 150th anniversary of the first lifeboat on Anglesey (1828 – 1978). This was founded by the Reverend James Williams and his wife Frances after they witnessed the wreck of the Irish Packet 'Alert' which drifted onto West Mouse killing 145 people in 1823. The Reverend and his wife watched helplessly from this headland as the packet ship sank, leaving only seven survivors.

James and Frances devoted the rest of their lives to the formation of the Anglesey Association for the Preservation of Life from Shipwreck. James was awarded the first RNLI Gold medal in Wales, after playing a major role in the rescue of sailors from the vessel 'Active', wrecked in Cemaes Bay in 1835. Ironically, it was not at the helm of his lifeboat but from the shore, where he used his horse to get deeper into the surf and throw a grappling iron to the wreck, thus saving the lives of five men.

Follow the lane which soon passes beside the lagoon to your left. At a T junction turn left and at the next junction turn left again. Walk along the lane for about ½ mile (ignore a left turn to the Cemlyn Bay car park) and turn left into an access road which leads to a small stone farm ('Felin Gafnan'). Go through the gate passing the farm on your left and join the coastal path again. Turn right now and retrace the outward journey to complete the walk.

Ynys y Fydlyn

Distance: *3¹/₂ miles*

A walk visiting a beautiful and remote rocky cove followed by a section of dramatic coastline. Moderately strenuous, the return is made on quiet lanes and good footpaths.

Start: Take the A5025 north from Valley and turn left to the village of Rhydwyn just before Llanrhyddlad. Take the lane which runs northwest from Rhydwyn for about 2 miles. Where the lane bends sharp right, turn left into a small car park. Access along the coast on this route is closed between 14th September and 1st February.
Grid ref. 303 914. (Landranger 114, Explorer 262).

The walk

1. From the car park go through the gate and follow the track beside conifer woods on the right. Where this becomes indistinct keep straight ahead and join a well worn track further down near woods on the right again. Follow this track down to the beautiful little cove at Ynys y Fydlyn.

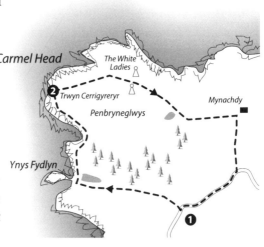

53

Ynys y Fydlyn

In 1986 the National Trust bought 412 acres of the Mynachdy Estate with support from the Countryside Commission. This enabled a large section of wild coastline to be opened to the public where previously there had been few public rights of way.

Much of this land is now managed as a pheasant rearing area, with a winter shoot providing the main income for the estate. Because of this, access to footpaths within the estate is only permitted between 1 February and 14 September.

This little cove with its shingle beach, crystal clear water and fine rock scenery is one of the most attractive locations on this part of the island. The remoteness of the cove probably means that you will have it to yourself, although you may be watched from the woods by thousands of young pheasants specially bred for the winter shoot.

At low tide it is easy enough to get onto Ynys y Fydlyn, from where you will be able to enjoy a fine view of the dramatic rock scenery which surrounds the cove. To the left, there is a huge sea cave and a marshy area which backs the bay (known as Llyn y Fydlyn). This was once a small inlet from the sea but has now become separated and has almost dried out. Both these features have been formed by the action of waves over the centuries, particularly during the winter months when strong westerly gales persist. Large sea caves like this can also be seen at North Stack on the exposed west coast of Holy Island.

Beyond Carmel Head, the lighthouse on The Skerries warns shipping of the treacherous rocks and reefs which reach out from Anglesey's northwestern tip. This coastline has been a hazard to shipping for centuries and has been responsible for literally hundreds of wrecks. One of the most notable was that of the 'Mary', a 52 foot sloop which sank after hitting the rocks in thick fog in 1675. The 'Mary' came from Amsterdam and was presented to Charles II, making it the first royal yacht. The 'Hudiksvall', a Swedish barque was wrecked on Ynys y Fydlyn in 1890 and the crew of 116 were forced to lash themselves to the upper rails until the Holyhead Lifeboat came to their aid. All lives were saved.

Turn right along the shingle beach and go through the gate at the far end which takes you onto the permissive footpath to Penbryneglwys (only accessible between 1 February and 14 September each year). Walk diagonally up the bank at first, then turn sharp left and walk across the top of the high cliffs overlooking the island. The path becomes indistinct from here but curves away from the cliffs for a short distance before turning left again just before the woods.

At the top of a small rocky ridge overlooking a crag-lined inlet, do not be tempted to drop directly to a kissing gate in the fence below, instead, bear left slightly until you reach a wooden post marking the path. A right turn here will bring you to the kissing gate seen from the top of the bank. Bear left up the field to a second kissing gate in the wall. Follow the faint path to the rocky top of Trwyn Cerrigyreryr (about 400 yards).

2. From Trwyn Cerrigyreryr walk east over the featureless slopes of Penbryneglwys aiming just to the right of the beacon on the small island of West Mouse but keeping to the left of the rounded flat summit of Penbrynyreglwys.

A Roman watchtower is thought to have existed somewhere on the rounded hilltop to the right. It is believed to have been used in conjunction with the similar structure on Holyhead Mountain to guard the approach to the harbour where the remains of the small coastal fort still stand in the centre of Holyhead.

Further on, if the weather is clear, aim for the point at which the horizon meets the hillside of Penbryneglwys. Continue across the hillside until the ruins of mine workings come into view. The chimney is the first to be seen along with a view east along the north coast.

The mines date from a period of prosperity in the copper industry during the eighteenth century, although there is evidence of mining here in prehistoric times.

Pass the chimney on your left and pick up a grass track which contours the hillside to a gate beyond the 'White Ladies' beacons (the tall white pillars). Beyond the gate, follow the track through a larger grazing field to a gate and stone steps over the wall in the far corner. Bear half-right through a smaller field to a ladder stile about 150 yards away and head left along a track which soon curves to the right around a small artificial pool backed by conifer woods. Follow the track towards farm buildings at Mynachdy and pass into the farmyard. Turn right immediately and walk down the access road to the lane. Turn right along the lane and return to the car park at point 1.

Llanfachraeth

Distance: *6 miles*

An unusual walk on quiet lanes and along wide open beaches to the mouth of a small tidal estuary. Field paths lead back along the marsh edge to the village of Llanfachraeth. Easy level walking for much of the way.

Start: Begin the walk in the village of Llanfachraeth situated 3 miles north of Valley on the A5025. Park at the northern end of the village where there is a loop of the old road opposite the church. *Grid ref. 314 832 (Landranger 114, Explorer 262).*

The walk

1. Immediately opposite the lay-by and just past the large house beside the church turn left onto a signed footpath. This is enclosed at first with a high wall to the left. After about 50 yards a small gate on the right leads into a field. Walk directly through the field to enter a lane by a kissing gate and finger post. Turn left along the lane and walk for about 1 mile to Llanfwrog church.

Walk past the church on your left and after about 150 yards turn left into the signed lane to 'Penrhyn'. Ignore the lane on the right after about 500 yards ('Porth Tywyn Sandy Beach'), instead, continue along the road almost to the beach at Porth Penrhyn-mawr.

2. Here, within a hundred yards of the beach the road forks. Keep right on the concrete road for 100 yards or so before turning left across a small area of grass to join an unsurfaced track with a bungalow to the left. Follow this track along the back of the bay, then rise towards a farm.

Llanfwrog church

Do not follow the track left into the farm, instead cross the stile straight ahead and walk directly up the following field. The next stile is not in the field corner but in the middle of the top hedge line. Keep left in the following field and walk down towards a farm on the edge of the next bay.

Despite a modest height of just 70 feet there is a fine view of the surrounding countryside from this little hill. To your right, across the wide sweep of Holyhead Bay the Irish ferries can be seen entering and leaving Holyhead harbour, whilst the chimney of the aluminium works provides one of the most visible landmarks on this side of the island. Directly ahead the distant peaks of Yr Eifl (The Rivals) can be seen on the horizon with the higher summits of Snowdonia further to the left.

Keep to the left of the farm passing through a gap in the hedge, then bear half-right to a ladder stile before outbuildings. Go through the gate here and turn left along the track. At the end of the track turn right at a T junction and walk down onto the beach. Turn left here and walk along the sand for almost 1 mile.

3. After passing a house almost on the sand, look for a stile and gate on the left (about 300 yards past the house). This leads onto a track which heads towards a ruined farm building. About 50 yards along the track turn right over a stile, then bear left along the edge of fields. The right of way is not visible on the ground initially, but cuts through an area of heather covered sand dunes to an embankment used to prevent flooding of the fields to the left.

The name of nearby Llanfachraeth, which means 'church at the little beach or inlet', undoubtedly refers to this small tidal estuary where Afon Alaw enters the sea at Holyhead Bay.

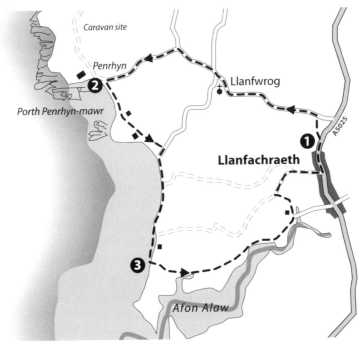

Afon Alaw is linked in folklore to the sad story of Branwen, one of the collection of traditional Welsh stories known as the Mabinogion. The tale, which is though to date from about 1060, concerns Bran a Welsh prince and his beautiful sister Branwen. Bran is approached by the king of Ireland for the hand of his sister in marriage. The match is agreed between the two rulers and Branwen travels back to her new home in Ireland. Things do not go well for Branwen in Ireland though; the king turns against her on account of a trick played on him in Wales. She is imprisoned and forced to labour long hours in the kitchens. Despite all communication being cut with Wales she manages to get a letter to her brother at Caernarfon by means of a starling which she has trained during her ordeal. The result is war between Wales and Ireland and many battles are fought before Branwen is released.

Stepping once more onto Welsh soil here at the mouth of Afon Alaw with what remained of her brother's army (just seven knights!) she fell to her knees and declared, "woe is me that ever I was born: two good islands have been laid waste because of me!" With that she lay down and died of a broken heart. Her body was carried inland along the course of the river where a mound was raised over her grave.

In the fields near the outflow from Llyn Alaw five or six miles upstream from here a mound known as 'Bedd Branwen' or 'Branwen's Grave' can still be seen and is the supposed location of her burial. The mound is certainly of great antiquity, in fact it was already ancient when this story was written. In 1813 it was excavated and a Bronze Age urn with the remains of cremated bones found at its centre.

Cross a stile at the far end of the sea wall and bear half-left through the bracken. Aim just to the right of a small stone farm building and eventually pick up a faint track which will take you to a ladder stile on the left. Bear diagonally-left across the next field to the outside corner of a field on the left. There is a waymark here and a field to the right which is marshy and frequently inundated by high tides. Keep left along the field edge to a ladder stile which leads onto a short access track. After a few yards turn right over a second ladder stile and keep along the fence to a stile in the lower right-hand corner. This leads onto

Looking across Holyhead Bay near the mouth of Afon Alaw

the marsh edge and may be flooded during certain high tides (if so either wait for the water to fall or return across the field and turn right to the lane. Follow this lane back to Llanfachraeth).

The path along the marsh edge stays close to the hedge and fence on your left. Further on a stile leads into a small field and a second stile takes you back onto the marsh edge again. Continue to a kissing gate beside a farm on the left. Turn right here then left immediately before the old bridge onto a signed footpath which runs beside a tidal pool on the right. Do not cross the stone footbridge over the pool, instead, continue straight ahead to stone steps over the wall which lead into a small field. Keep left to a stile in the corner and in the following field bear half-left to a stile and gate which lead into a narrow lane. Turn right and follow the lane to Llanfachraeth. A left turn here will take you back to the lay-by opposite the church.

Holyhead Mountain

Distance: *5 miles*

This walk visits one of the most spectacular walking areas on the island with the highest sea cliffs in North Wales and the option to visit island's highest point. Footpaths are good throughout.

Start: Begin the walk at the 'Breakwater Country Park' in Holyhead, located at the northwestern end of the seafront, at the end of 'Beach Road'. Start the walk at the little visitor centre. *Grid ref. 226 832 (Landranger 114, Explorer 262).*

The walk

1. Cross the car park to pass through a gap in the wall and walk ahead along a gravel path (signed for 'St Cybi Circular Walk') passing a pool on the right. Go through a kissing gate onto a track and turn left. In about 50 yards bear right through a kissing gate beside a field gate. The path goes ahead through rough grass and gorse towards a large quarry face. As you approach the cliff face the path curves right to a point overlooking the sea with a wide view back to Holyhead harbour. Bear left here onto a pitched path which contours the slopes. Stay on the pitched path ignoring minor paths here and there and soon you will be able to see along the coast to North Stack. Pass the little magazine building (keeping it below you) and continue up the steep pitched path. At a path junction bear right and follow the path down to North Stack.

   As you approach the house at North Stack a track comes in sharply from the left which you will use to continue the walk.

Overlooking Gogarth Bay

Anyone with a head for heights can walk down to the end of the rocks to the left of the boundary wall for an impressive view of the cliff scenery. Looking back you will see the enormous cavern beneath the house which will eventually separate the rock you are now standing on from the main cliff to create another stack. To the right there is a view along Gogarth Bay where a number of high grade rock climbs have been recorded. Climbers can often be seen dotting the face.

2. Walk back to the house and turn right up the track until it begins to level and there is a junction of paths. Take the signed coastal path which bears right here. This has been stone pitched and rises in a series of steps up towards Holyhead Mountain. Ignore minor paths on the right as you rise as these are paths mainly used by rock climbers to reach the cliffs below

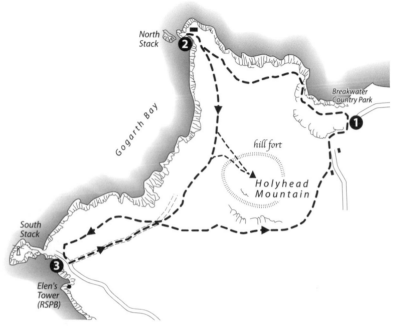

Over to the right there is a superb view across Gogarth Bay towards South Stack.

Continue until the path levels with Holyhead Mountain ahead. Make a slight drop to a broad col. (A left fork here will take you to the summit of Holyhead Mountain. If you take the summit detour return to the col to continue the walk.) Keep ahead on the coastal path which will take you over the shoulder of the mountain towards South Stack.

Soon communication dishes come into view. Keep ahead and, immediately adjacent to the dishes (on the right), bear right off the main path onto a narrower path which leads to the tarmac access road to the dishes. Turn left along the road for about 30 yards then bear right onto a stoney footpath passing close to brick buildings on the left beneath a radio mast. This path bends right, drops slightly, then rises to pass along a rounded heather ridge with a small pool down to the left. Soon you will find yourself in a dramatic position overlooking South Stack Lighthouse from beside the ruins of the old telegraph station. Head half-left from here to reach the road head directly above the lighthouse.

South Stack is one of the most spectacular locations on Anglesey and its lighthouse is probably one of the most photographed in Wales. Construction of a beacon here was begun in 1798 and cost over £12,000.

South Stack Lighthouse

The structure was finished and its oil lamp first lit on 9 February 1809. The present structure was automated in 1984 when the keepers were withdrawn. Today it is monitored by computer link from the Trinity House Operations Centre in Harwich, Essex

3. Turn left along the road for about 100 yards or so and turn left up a signed tarmac/concrete road. At a crossing track take the path ahead and at a fork keep ahead again soon passing the brick buildings passed earlier. At the next junction (below the 'dishes' again), bear right. This path takes you close below the crags of Holyhead Mountain then bears right. Keep left at a fork and rise slightly onto the rocky shoulder of the mountain ignoring a track on the right which leads to a small quarry. At the next junction keep ahead contouring past small wall-enclosed fields on the right.

As Holyhead comes into view the path enters walled enclosures. At a cross paths keep ahead. Soon there is a wide view of the breakwater reaching out into the bay. At a junction of access roads turn left and left again at a T junction. At the road end bear left along a grass path (adjacent to a house 'Cornish'). At a fork in 50 yards or so turn right soon passing beside a wire-link fence on the left. At a T junction turn left down steps and left again to return to the Breakwater Country Park to complete the walk.

Penrhyn Mawr

Distance: *8¹/₄ miles*

Superb walking around one of the few lowland heaths on the island. Footpaths are excellent and there are wide views to South Stack and across Caernarfon Bay to the Lleyn and Snowdonia. A series of smaller headlands and coves continue the theme of the walk followed by an inland loop through farmland.

Start: There is free parking at Penrhyn Mawr, a large open heather covered headland accessed from a short lane between Trearddur and South Stack.
Grid ref. 216 803 (Landranger 114, Explorer 262).

The walk

1. At the back of the car park there is a fingerpost indicating the coastal path both to the left and right. Take the right-hand option heading in the direction of South Stack Lighthouse. At a crossing path turn left heading southwest. At the coast bear left and follow the coastline all the way around the headland of Penrhyn Mawr. Pass round the back of Porth Ruffydd and keep following the coast bearing inland slightly at the rocky head of Dinas to go through a kissing gate. Walk round the grassy headland, passing through another gate to join a narrow path heading towards a caravan park. Join the path to Porth Dafarch beach. Cross the bay and bear right onto the signed coastal path again.

Walk around the headland and as you approach a house cross a wooden footbridge and stile and walk along an enclosed path to join the drive to a house on the right. Turn left up the drive to the road. Turn right and walk along the road for approximately 500 yards

2. Turn left down the access road to 'Isallt Fawr'. Pass houses on the left and at the end of the drive a footpath continues ahead to a ladder stile into fields. Cross the stile and walk along the right-hand field edges to an access road with houses on the right. Turn right here and walk along the access road to a T junction with a tarmac lane. Turn left along the lane and after about 100 yards take the signed field path on the right. Follow the path, which is enclosed at first, to enter a large field. Bear right through the field to a kissing gate in the far corner near bungalows. Go ahead to join an estate road and turn left.

At a T junction at the end of the road, turn left again and look for a signed footpath on the right. Turn right over the ladder stile and walk around the right-hand field edge. At a stile on the right cross over and walk ahead to a ladder stile by a gate. Cross the stile and follow the well worn footpath through an area of

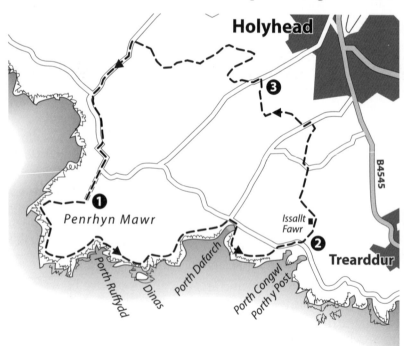

Looking north from Penrhyn Mawr to South Stack Lighthouse

rocks and gorse. Keep to the most obvious footpath (marked by the 'St Cybi Circular Walk' symbol although many are missing at the time of writing) ignoring minor footpaths on either side. Where Holyhead Mountain comes into view with a bungalow a field or so ahead, bear right over flat rocks—initially in the direction of a distant church tower in Holyhead. Don't go into smaller fields on the right, keep ahead between gorse bushes until you reach a bungalow beyond a fence. Bear left along the fence in front of the bungalow to a gate into a lane.

3. Turn left up the lane to a stile and sign on the right. Go over the stile and walk ahead to a gap in the wall/hedge, then ahead again with Holyhead Mountain ahead to a stile in an area of gorse. Cross the stile and continue through the area of gorse and flat rocks on a visible footpath.

At a wall and kissing gate, don't go through the gate, instead turn left to a stile in the corner. Go over this stile and follow the path ahead with a wall on the right. Pass a farmhouse on the right continuing ahead. Soon the footpath bears left to pass below some small rock outcrops on the left. After the outcrops go through a kissing gate on the right and keep ahead on a good footpath with Holyhead Mountain ahead again. In the field corner bear left with the fence.

Near a farm on the right, continue ahead to a gap in the fence (waymarker) on the right. Go through the gap and keep ahead with Holyhead Mountain ahead again and a farm on the right. Soon a waymarker post directs you right to a ladder stile. Go over the stile then bear left through a small field past a gorse covered bank on the right. Walk ahead to a gateway with an overhead power cable post beside it. Go through the gate and follow a path up the following field towards a farm. Walk ahead between the outbuildings (but to the left of the farmhouse) to a gate into a road.

Turn left along the road for about ¹/₂ mile.

Opposite a lane on the right (this is the first lane you will meet and leads to South Stack), turn left up the bank onto a new permissive footpath (signed for the coastal path) which runs parallel to the road. At the end of the path join the road for about ¹/₄ mile before turning right down the access road to Penrhyn Mawr to complete the walk

Cymyran

Distance: 6¼ miles

Attractive walking around the tidal estuary separating Holy Island from Anglesey on a mixture of old lanes, tidal roads and the coastal path. Paths are generally good throughout.

Start: Free parking is available in the beach car park at Cymyran, 2 miles south of Caergeiliog.
Grid ref 297 755 (Landranger 114, Explorer 262).

The walk

1. Walk back along the track to join the tarmac road near the little cafe. Continue along the road until, just before the road goes over the railway, there is an access track on the left immediately after a stone house (opposite a road on the right). Turn left here, walk down the access road and just before a large cottage (about 350 yards), turn right over a rough stone stile into a small field. In the corner of the field climb over an old iron ladder stile and turn left to a second stile. Bear right towards farm buildings to join a farm track. Turn left and walk down the track to a quiet lane which crosses the head of a marsh covered tidal creek.

2. Turn right for about 50 yards, then bear left onto a tidal road which follows the edge of mud flats to a point where another lane comes down onto the marsh. (If the tide is high it may not be possible to follow this road, but a high tide option exists along the top of the bank to the right.) Walk up the lane for almost 1 mile.

3. Close to the expressway and immediately after crossing a small river, turn left down the access road to 'Tyddyn-y-Cob'. This road runs beside a large pool on the left and as you approach an embankment containing the pool, bends sharply right to the house. Turn left here, cross the embankment to steps over the wall. Keep along the right-hand field edge crossing a wide stone wall in the corner by stone steps, then keep ahead in the following field for about 80 yards and turn right over a stone footbridge and steps. Cross a wooden walkway over boggy ground and continue straight ahead up the field to enter a quiet lane.

Turn left and after a few yards turn right into a lane immediately after a cottage. Pass a house on the left, and just after a gate with the sign 'Glan Rhyd Isaf' on it, bear right down to a ladder stile. Cross the field, over a double ladder stile, and then walk between two lines of telegraph poles to another ladder stile. After this turn right along a hedge to a ladder stile at 'Glan Rhyd Isaf'. The official line of the footpath carries on in front of the house and loops round in a circle to the shore, however it is recommended that you turn left down the drive straight to the shore.

From here, bear left for about 40 yards to a ladder stile on the left to join an attractive section of coastal path which

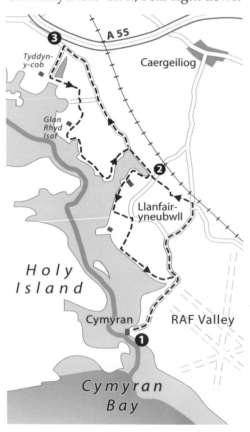

The coastal path near Glan Rhyd Isaf

overlooks the tidal estuary separating Anglesey from Holy Island. This is probably the most enjoyable section of the walk (photo above).

The shallow tidal creek which separates Holy Island from Anglesey almost dries out at low tide and a number of tidal routes crossed the sands before the modern roads were built. Prior to the building of the Stanley Embankment which now carries the A5, travellers on the Holyhead road en-route to Ireland followed a tidal route across the sands to the north of Valley. This crossing, along with the detour which could be made to Pont-rhydbont or the Four Mile Bridge, is shown on the maps of John Ogilby published in 1675. By this time ships were regularly leaving Holyhead for Ireland and this previously quiet corner of Wales would have been busy with travellers.

Keep along the field edges until you pass a small building on the right. Soon after this, bear right through a gap in the hedge/ fence to join a muddy track at the mouth of a tidal creek. This is the creek visited earlier in the walk.

Turn right along the tidal road and return to the lane junction where you joined the tidal road earlier in the walk. Turn right along the lane and right again onto the signed coastal path.

In about 30 yards cross a ladder stile on the right and follow the path along the edge of fields and marsh on the right. Just before a cottage turn left away from the creek and follow the hedge on the right to a ladder stile. Cross the stile into a lane, turn right passing an access track and in about 20 yards turn right over a second stile into fields. Keep to the right-hand field edge initially, then to the right of aircraft landing lights. Eventually cross a ladder stile and bear half-left towards the little tea shack passed earlier. Cross a stile and turn right along the lane retracing outward journey.

Cymyran

Traeth Crigyll

Distance: *7½ miles*

An inland walk over a sandy common to a group of lakes with a return made along a vast sandy beach. Footpaths are generally good but sections across the common are indistinct.

Start: Park in a small lay-by just before 'The Anglesey Golf Club' at the northern end of Rhosneigr.
Grid ref 324 739 (Landranger 114, Explorer 262).

The walk

1. Walk along the road towards the golf club and turn left onto the signed footpath as you approach the clubhouse. The right of way passes the clubhouse before turning sharp left onto a footpath which heads for a footbridge over Afon Crigyll. Immediately after the bridge the path continues directly ahead on a raised bank towards a bridge under the railway. Turn right under the bridge and go through a gate. Turn left and follow a footpath across the golf course for about ¾ mile. As a rough guide, the path runs at about 2 o' clock to the railway on your left aiming a little to the right of the group of houses on the horizon (Llanfihangel yn Nhowyn).

Cross a narrow tarmac access road and continue ahead across Tywyn Trewan Common to Cerrig Cynrig, a farm near Llyn Traffwll. There is no specific path to follow here, but keep a fairly straight course making your way through the gorse bushes.

Tywyn Trewan Common is a vast area of wind blown sand covering layers of peat and marsh. Originally these marshes were inundated by tidal water and a number of lakes, now dried out, are known to have

75

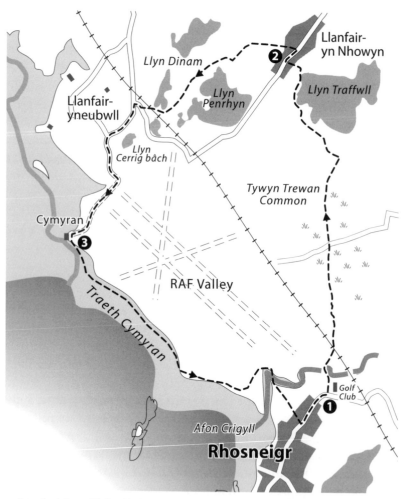

existed. A handful of lakes remain at the northern end of the common close to the village of Llanfihangel yn Nhowyn.

The western half of the common is now occupied by RAF Valley which opened on the 13 February 1941. Whatever your thoughts about the location of this air base, it is worth considering the possible outcome of an attempt made over 40 years earlier to build an explosives factory here. A local enquiry was held to decide whether or not the site was suitable. The proposed factory would have occupied 55 acres of the *common and employed over 300 men. Subsidiary factories were also planned for the production of soap. Fortunately this project was strongly opposed by a number of locals who had recently built hotels at nearby Rhosneigr in an attempt to develop the village's tourist trade. As a result the factory was never built.*

During the construction of an extension to one of the runways at the air base in 1943 one of the most remarkable Iron Age finds in the country was unearthed. It consisted of a large collection of ornaments, tools and weapons. There were even parts of a chariot found, in addition to large quantities of animal bones. The items are thought to have been deposited into what at that time would have been a shallow lake before the build up of the sand dunes. At first it was thought that these items had been lost in the marshes over a long period, but as their numbers grew it became apparent that such a vast quantity could only have been placed there intentionally.

The finds date from the second century BC to the middle of the first century AD and it is now believed that they were placed there as part of sacrificial rituals. By the time of the Roman invasion, Anglesey is known to have been the spiritual centre of the Druid religion in Europe and the dates of the later finds coincide with the abrupt end of the Druids at the hands of Suetonius' army, about AD 61.

If you have taken the correct route across the common there should be an old metal gate leading into fields on your approach to the farm mentioned earlier. Go through the gate and walk towards the farm along the field edge with the fence to your right. Adjacent to the farm a stile on the left takes you onto the farm access road. Turn right here and walk through the farmyard turning left over a stile into fields again at the back of the house. Keep left beside the fence and turn left again over a stile in the lower corner of the field. Walk along a raised footpath with a marshy field to the right and the water of Llyn Traffwll beyond, until you can turn right onto a similar raised footpath. Just before the lake, turn left through a metal gate.

Walk a short distance to a stile and footbridge. In the following field continue ahead until you pass under overhead cables—bear right here and follow the cables until the footpath becomes more distinct as it rises over a ridge of rock. Rise over the rock rib and keep right towards the lake. The path almost reaches the lake edge, then bears left passing a large split rock. Meet the overhead cables again and keep right crossing the stream at a tumbled down bridge. After a ladder stile turn right through gorse and pass through an area of large rocks. With the lake quite close on the right, though not always visible, make your way through the rocks to enter a small field by a stile with the houses of Llanfihangel yn Nhowyn up to the left. A stile and footbridge lead into a sloping field and the right of way takes a line half-left to a stile which leads into a farm access road. Turn left along the road and follow this to the main road through the village.

2. Turn right along the road and opposite the church turn left into a housing estate 'Ffordd Cerrig Mawr'. Walk through a development of MOD houses and along a track to a cottage 'Ysgubor Bach'. Go through a kissing gate to the left of the cottage and keep right along the field edge to a second kissing gate. In the following field keep to the edge again and just before houses turn right over a stile in the hedge. Walk across a small field to a stile and gate. Bear half-left now to a stile in the far corner of the field. Follow a well defined footpath through a rough area of heather and gorse between two lakes to a footbridge and wooden walkway. Immediately after the walkway bear right onto a signed footpath which rises slightly to overlook a small reed filled pool.

Aim for a ruined cottage to the right now which is approached via a footbridge. At the cottage turn left and walk towards the railway where a right turn before the lines will take you to a bridge. Cross the bridge, pass through a kissing gate and cut through a small field to the road. Turn right along the road and at the T junction in 80 yards or so turn left.

Follow the lane to the end of the tarmac where there is a small cafe and unofficial viewing area where aircraft from RAF Valley can be seen at very close quarters landing and taking off. A rough

Fighter planes training at RAF Valley

dirt road continues from here to a beach car park at Cymyran where there is a large house by the beach. Follow the road and at Cymyran walk down beside the house (on the right) onto the sand.

3. Turn left and walk along the beach for about 1³/₄ miles.

It was on this beach that Rhosneigr's most famous shipwreck occurred in March 1883. The ship in question was the 'Norman Court', *a tea-clipper and sister ship to more famous* 'Cutty Sark'. *She was built in 1869 and at the time of her final voyage was on the return journey from Java to Greenock on the Firth of the Clyde carrying 1,100 tons of sugar.*

On 29 March she was blown off course and became trapped in Cymyran Bay. All attempts to turn the ship around failed and she ran aground at 7pm with such force that half the rigging came down rendering the lifeboats useless. All attempts to launch the Rhosneigr lifeboat failed in the heavy seas and the crew were left clinging to the rigging until the following day. At first light another attempt to launch the lifeboat was made which almost ended in disaster when one of the crew was washed overboard.

By this time the crew of the Holyhead lifeboat had arrived by train and managed to reach the stricken ship in the Rhosneigr lifeboat, rescuing all but two of the crew who had died from exposure during the night. In all, twenty lives were saved.

The approach to Rhosneigr is blocked by Afon Crigyll. At low tide it is easy to paddle across the stream but if this does not appeal or the tide makes it impossible, bear left to a footbridge about ½ mile upstream. Beyond the bridge bear half-right into the village and at the main road turn left returning to the lay-by where the walk started.

Traeth Crigyll

Newborough Warren & Abermenai

Distance: *3¹/₂ or 6³/₄ miles*

This walk explores the extreme southern tip of the island—a wild expanse of wind-blown dunes, tidal sands and marshes. If you intend to complete the longer option to Abermenai Point, time the walk to coincide with a low or falling tide enabling you to cross the estuary safely. If you can not do this, the shorter walk can be completed safely at any state of the tide.

Start: Take the A4080 from Dwyran to Newborough. At Pen-lôn there is a small roundabout where a right turn continues to Newborough. Take the lane straight ahead which leads to a small car park by Llyn Rhos-Ddu.
Grid ref. 426 647 (Landranger 114, Explorer 263).

The walk

1. Turn left out of the car park and take the signed coastal path with the reeds of Llyn Rhos-Ddu to the right. After about 700 yards there is a small kissing gate on the left along with an information board and a grass farm track on the right. Turn left through the kissing gate and walk through the dunes of Newborough Warren National Nature Reserve for about 1¹/₂ miles. It is important that walkers keep to the right of way which is marked at frequent intervals by white posts.

Newborough Warren has been a sensitive and problematic area since Elizabethan times when over grazing resulted in the loss of valuable agricultural land beneath several metres of wind-blown sand. Today it provides a haven for wildlife being one of the largest sand dune systems in Britain. It is also designated as a national nature reserve in recognition of its rich flora and fauna.

Summer is the best time to visit the dunes when they are carpeted with wild flowers. Orchids are particularly notable and are often found growing in profusion. From June common spotted, pyramidal and marsh orchids are in flower. In July the dune hollows are full of marsh helleborines and the rarer dune helleborine can also be found. As the summer progresses and the orchids wither, delicate white wintergreen and grass of parnassus take their place and later purple flowered autumn gentian. The rich supply of nectar from the varied flowers attracts a wealth of insects including the distinctive red and black day-flying burnet moth.

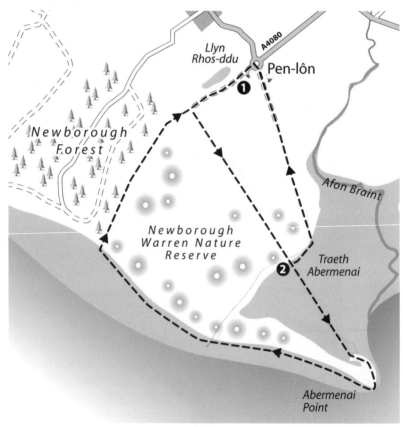

Newborough Warren

Also, look for cormorants and other sea birds. Ynys yr Adar ('Bird Island') near Ynys Llanddwyn supports over one per cent of the British breeding population of the Cormorant.

The area is equally special in winter when the mud flats and salt marshes are important wintering grounds for wildfowl and waders.

The path comes to an abrupt halt on the edge of the vast tidal sands of Traeth Abermenai.

Over on the mainland you will see the town of Caernarfon with its famous castle built by Edward I after his conquest of Wales in the thirteenth century. Behind the town, the skyline is filled with a

Sulptures at the start of the walk

panorama of Snowdonia's highest peaks, while to the west, the pointed tops of Yr Eifl peep over the dunes at Abermenai Point.

2. (Longer walk) If the water is low or falling you will have time to cross the estuary to Abermenai Point. Take a direct line aiming for the left-hand end of the distant line of sand dunes (about 1 mile). Do not ignore the warning given at the beginning of this chapter regarding suitable times for crossing the sands to Abermenai Point.

Prior to the bridging of the Menai Strait by Thomas Telford in 1826, a number of ferries crossed to the mainland from Abermenai Point. The ferry which served this southern end of the Strait gave the islanders access to the market at Caernarfon. The dangerous nature of the crossing is illustrated by the fact that several ferry boats came to grief with many fatalities.

Perhaps the most tragic was that which occurred on 5 December

1785. The ferry left Caernarfon with 55 passengers on board about one hour before low tide. Halfway across, the boat hit a sand bank, tipped over and could not be re-floated. When the tide turned she began taking in water leaving the passengers stranded on the shrinking sand bar in the middle of the channel until one by one they were swept away to perish in the freezing water. Only one person survived, a man named Hugh Williams from Aberffraw who was washed ashore two hours later.

From Abermenai Point walk northwest along the beach towards Ynys Llanddwyn, a route which lies outside the restricted area of the nature reserve (2¾ miles). At the edge of the conifers of the Newborough Forest (before you reach Ynys Llanddwyn), turn right onto the signed coastal path which will take you back to the car park to complete the route.

2. (Shorter walk) If you have any doubts about crossing the sands to Abermenai, or prefer a shorter walk, turn left and follow the path along the edge of the estuary for about 500 yards and look for a post which marks the right of way back to Pen-lôn. Turn left here and follow the path across the dunes again to join a lane by houses and a picnic area. Continue straight ahead along the lane and at the roundabout turn left to complete the walk.

The unusual sculptures in the car park depict bundles of marram grass which were gathered locally for a thriving basket making industry carried out in the nineteenth century.

Mara Books www.marabooks.co.uk

Mara Books publish a range of walking books for Cheshire
and North Wales and have the following list to date.

North Wales

Circular Walks in the Conwy Valley

ISBN 0 9522409 7 1. A collection of 18 circular
walks which explore the varied scenery of this
beautiful valley from the Great Orme to Betws-y-
Coed.

A pocket guide to Snowdon

ISBN 1 902512 04 9. A guide to all Snowdon's
recognised routes of ascent, from the six 'Classic
Paths' to the many lesser known and less
frequented routes.

Walking in Snowdonia Volume 1

ISBN 1 902512 06 5. A series of circular walks
exploring the beautiful and dramatic valleys in
the northern half of the Snowdonia National
Park.

Coastal Walks around Anglesey Volume 1

ISBN 0 9522409 6 3. A collection of 15 walks which
explore the varied scenery of Anglesey's beautiful
coastline.

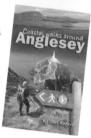

Walking the Isle of Anglesey Coastal Path

ISBN 1 902512 13 8. The official guide for the Isle of Anglesey Coastal Path. Full colour in English and Welsh.

Walking on the Lleyn Peninsula

ISBN 1 902512 00 6. A collection of 16 circular walks which explore the wild and beautiful coastline and hills of the Lleyn Peninsula.

Walking in the Clwydian Hills

ISBN 1 902512 09 X. A collection of 18 circular walks exploring the Clwydian Range Area of Outstanding Natural Beauty (AONB).

Walking in the Vale of Clwyd and Denbigh Moors

ISBN 1 902512 08 1. A collection of 18 circular walks exploring the undiscovered country between the Clwydian Hills and the Conwy Valley.

Circular walks along the Offa's Dyke Path

—Volume 1 Prestatyn to Welshpool
ISBN 1 902512 01 4.

—Volume 2 Welshpool to Hay-on-Wye
ISBN 1 902512 07 3.

The first two volumes in a series of three which sample some of the finest sections of this well known national trail.

The Mountain Men
ISBN 1 902512 11 1. This book tells the story of the pioneer rock climbers in Snowdonia in the closing decades of the nineteenth century until the outbreak of World War II.

Cheshire

Circular Walks along the Sandstone Trail
ISBN 1 902512 10 3. The Sandstone Trail is Cheshire's best known and most popular walking route. This book gives a complete route description along with 12 circular walks covering the entire trail.

A Walker's Guide to the Wirral Shore Way
ISBN 1 902512 05 7. A linear walk of 23 miles following the old coastline between Chester and Hoylake.

Circular Walks along the Gritstone Trail and Mow Cop Trail
ISBN 0 9522409 4 7. A route which follows Cheshire's eastern border along the edge of the Peak District. Following the same format as the Sandstone Trail book—a full description for both trails is combined with 12 circular walks.

Circular Walks in Wirral
ISBN 1 902512 02 2. A collection of 15 circular walks in the coast and countryside of Wirral.

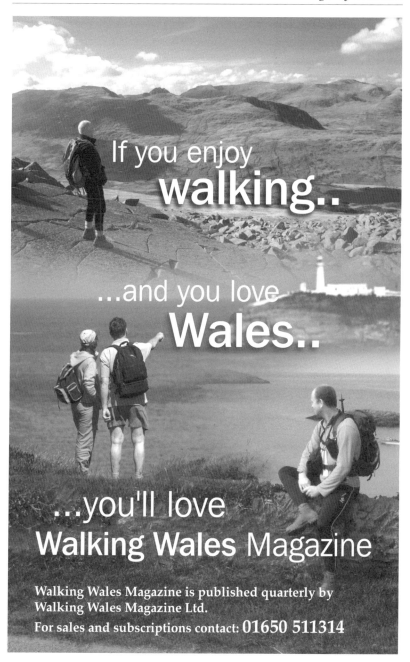